Key Stage 2 Maths Practice Papers TEACHER BOOK

12x Maths Tests: Arithmetic and Reasoning

Contents

Arithmetic Paper 1:

Test 1	4
Test 2	18
Test 3	32
Test 4	46

Reasoning Paper 2:

Test 1	60
Test 2	70
Test 3	80
Test 4	89

Reasoning Paper 3:

Test 1	98
Test 2	108
Test 3	118
Test 4	127

Answers:

Arithmetic	136
Reasoning	138

National curriculum tests

Key Stage 2

Test 1

Mathematics

Paper 1: arithmetic

First name					
Middle name					
Last name					
Date of birth	Day		Month		Year	
School name					

Total Marks	/ 40

Instructions

You **may not** use a calculator to answer any questions in this test.

Questions and answers

You have **30 minutes** to complete this test.

Work as quickly and as carefully as you can.

Put your answer in the box for each question.

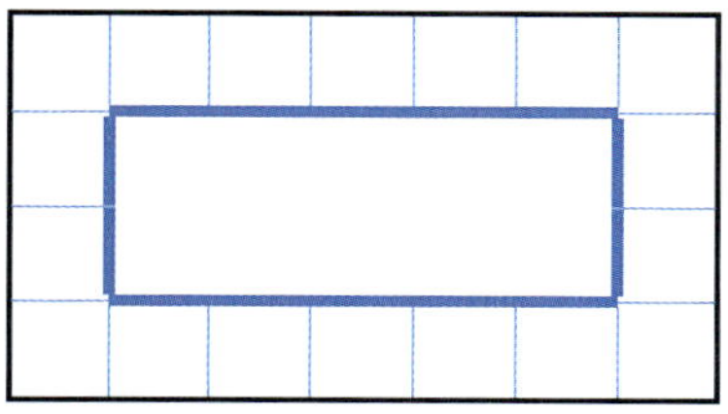

For questions expressed as common fractions, you should give your answers as common fractions.

All other answers should be given as either whole or decimal numbers.

If you cannot do one of the questions, **go on to the next one.** You can come back to it later if you have time.

If you finish before the end, **go back and check your work.**

Marks

The number under each box at the side of the page tells you the maximum number of marks for each question.

In this test, long division and long multiplication questions are worth **2 marks each.** You will be awarded 2 marks for a correct answer.

You may get 1 mark for showing a formal method.

All other questions are worth **1 mark each.**

If you finish before the end, go back and check your work.

1

843 + 100 =

1 mark

2

145 x 4 =

1 mark

3

7.3 + 0.2 =

1 mark

4

34 x 4 =

1 mark

5

1,284 + 492 =

1 mark

6

84 ÷ 7 =

1 mark

7

591 - 8 =

1 mark

8

1.6 + 0.06 =

1 mark

9

6 x 3 x 4 =

1 mark

10

$\frac{5}{8} - \frac{2}{8} =$

1 mark

11

$360 \div 8 =$

1 mark

12

$1.74 \times 100 =$

1 mark

13

$6^2 =$

1 mark

14

25,000 - 200 =

1 mark

15

200 x 200 =

1 mark

16

2,136 ÷ 12 =

1 mark

17

25% of 1,264 =

1 mark

18

1.82 x 4 =

1 mark

19

$\frac{2}{7} + \frac{1}{7} =$

1 mark

20

4,841 + 9,720 =

1 mark

21

5,965 ÷ 5 =

1 mark

22

6 - 4.27 =

1 mark

23

$$\begin{array}{r} 2\ 8 \\ \times \quad 6\ 1 \\ \hline \end{array}$$

Show your method

2 marks

24

13.2 - 4.45 =

1 mark

25

3,185 ÷ 13 =

1 mark

26

$\frac{1}{3} \times \frac{1}{9} =$

1 mark

27

85% of 260 =

1 mark

28

$139{,}674 - 56{,}388 =$

1 mark

29

$$\begin{array}{r} 4\;8\;2 \\ \times \quad 4\;5 \\ \hline \end{array}$$

Show your method

2 marks

30

$15 \times 1\frac{3}{8} =$

1 mark

31

$18 - 2 \times 3 =$

1 mark

32

$\frac{2}{3} \div 5 =$

1 mark

33

$1\frac{2}{5} - \frac{1}{3} =$

1 mark

34

$32\overline{)4704}$

Show your method

2 marks

35

$\frac{1}{8} + \frac{3}{4} =$

1 mark

36

$28\overline{)1344}$

Show your method

2 marks

National curriculum tests

Key Stage 2

Test 2

Mathematics

Paper 1: arithmetic

First name						
Middle name						
Last name						
Date of birth	Day		Month		Year	
School name						

Total Marks	/ 40

Instructions

You **may not** use a calculator to answer any questions in this test.

Questions and answers

You have **30 minutes** to complete this test.

Work as quickly and as carefully as you can.

Put your answer in the box for each question.

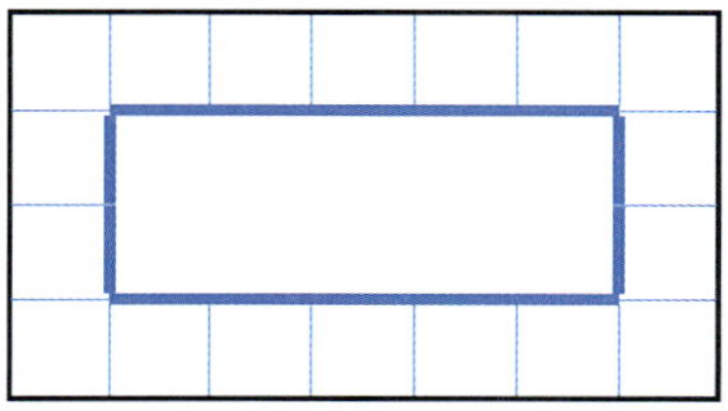

For questions expressed as common fractions, you should give your answers as common fractions.

All other answers should be given as either whole or decimal numbers.

If you cannot do one of the questions, **go on to the next one.** You can come back to it later if you have time.

If you finish before the end, **go back and check your work.**

Marks

The number under each box at the side of the page tells you the maximum number of marks for each question.

In this test, long division and long multiplication questions are worth **2 marks each.** You will be awarded 2 marks for a correct answer.

You may get 1 mark for showing a formal method.

All other questions are worth **1 mark each.**

If you finish before the end, go back and check your work.

1

32 x 5 =

1 mark

2

542 - 11 =

1 mark

3

1,632 x 4 =

1 mark

4 $8.2 + 1.6 =$

1 mark

5 $293 + 10 =$

1 mark

6 $5,321 + 427 =$

1 mark

7

12 x 11 =

1 mark

8

36 ÷ 4 ÷ 3 =

1 mark

9

1.3 + 2.65 =

1 mark

10

$\frac{6}{8} - \frac{3}{8} =$

1 mark

11

$\frac{1}{3} + \frac{1}{3} =$

1 mark

12

680 ÷ 8 =

1 mark

13

3.61 x 100 =

1 mark

14

2,916 ÷ 9 =

1 mark

15

8^2 =

1 mark

16

23 + 1.16 =

1 mark

17

262 x 100 =

1 mark

18

32,000 - 300 =

1 mark

19 15% of 3,500 =

1 mark

20 3.41 x 5 =

1 mark

21 72 ÷ 9 =

1 mark

22

12.2 - 2.33 =

1 mark

23

$$\begin{array}{r} 41 \\ \times\ 23 \\ \hline \end{array}$$

Show your method

2 marks

24

6,214 + 7,449 =

1 mark

25

65,234 - 22,751 =

1 mark

26

$$15\overline{)6150}$$

Show your method

2 marks

27

$\frac{1}{3} \times \frac{2}{5} =$

1 mark

28

40% of 60 =

1 mark

29

2,375 - 102 =

1 mark

30

$\frac{1}{2} \div 4 =$

1 mark

31

$12 \times 1\frac{2}{5} =$

1 mark

32

$36 + 12 \times 6 =$

1 mark

33

$\frac{3}{8} \div 4 =$

1 mark

34

$$\begin{array}{r} 463 \\ \times \quad 21 \\ \hline \end{array}$$

Show your method

2 marks

35

$$51\overline{)2142}$$

Show your method

2 marks

36

$$\frac{1}{6} + \frac{1}{4} =$$

1 mark

National curriculum tests

Key Stage 2

Test 3

Mathematics

Paper 1: arithmetic

First name					
Middle name					
Last name					
Date of birth	Day		Month		Year
School name					

Total Marks	/ 40

Instructions

You **may not** use a calculator to answer any questions in this test.

Questions and answers

You have **30 minutes** to complete this test.

Work as quickly and as carefully as you can.

Put your answer in the box for each question.

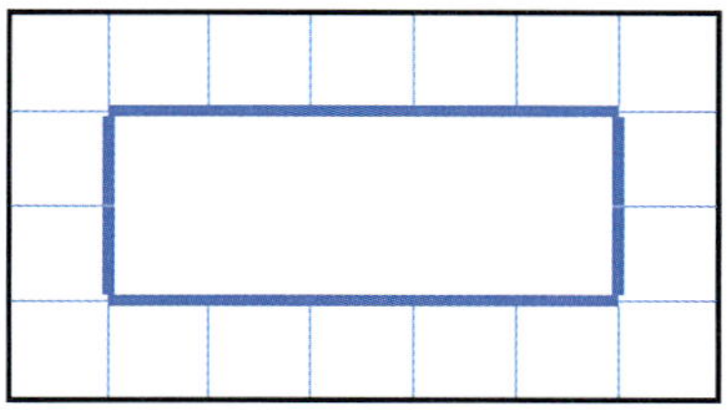

For questions expressed as common fractions, you should give your answers as common fractions.

All other answers should be given as either whole or decimal numbers.

If you cannot do one of the questions, **go on to the next one.** You can come back to it later if you have time.

If you finish before the end, **go back and check your work.**

Marks

The number under each box at the side of the page tells you the maximum number of marks for each question.

In this test, long division and long multiplication questions are worth **2 marks each.** You will be awarded 2 marks for a correct answer.

You may get 1 mark for showing a formal method.

All other questions are worth **1 mark each.**

If you finish before the end, go back and check your work.

1

100 ÷ 10 =

1 mark

2

5.2 + 0.7 =

1 mark

3

7 x 8 =

1 mark

4

361 x 6 =

1 mark

5

4,607 - 1,000 =

1 mark

6

38 x 7 =

1 mark

7

2,641 - 697 =

1 mark

8

25% of 340 =

1 mark

9

365 + 12 =

1 mark

10

4.5 + 0.18 =

1 mark

11

36,000 - 400 =

1 mark

12

6 x 2 x 9 =

1 mark

13

$\frac{1}{8} + \frac{5}{8} =$

1 mark

14

1,722 ÷ 7 =

1 mark

15

3.46 x 1,000 =

1 mark

16

$11^2 =$

1 mark

17

$\frac{8}{12} - \frac{3}{12} =$

1 mark

18

$1{,}408 \div 11 =$

1 mark

19 $\frac{1}{5} \times \frac{2}{3} =$

1 mark

20 $2.45 \times 3 =$

1 mark

21 $\frac{1}{2} + \frac{1}{8} =$

1 mark

22

6,751 + 9,102 =

1 mark

23

6,222 ÷ 3 =

1 mark

24

12.3 - 7.43 =

1 mark

25

15 - 2.41

1 mark

26

$$\begin{array}{r} 68 \\ \times\ 18 \\ \hline \end{array}$$

Show your method

2 marks

27

24 + 8 ÷ 2 =

1 mark

28

$14\overline{)3430}$

Show your method

2 marks

29

$14 \times 1\frac{3}{4} =$

1 mark

30

30% of 160 =

1 mark

31

621,841 - 53,174 =

1 mark

32

$$\begin{array}{r} 4\,3\,1 \\ \times \quad 6\,2 \\ \hline \end{array}$$

Show your method

2 marks

33

$\frac{6}{7} \div 3 =$

1 mark

34

$$18\overline{)1332}$$

Show your method

2 marks

35

$$1\frac{2}{5} - \frac{1}{3} =$$

1 mark

36

$$\frac{4}{5} \div 3 =$$

1 mark

National curriculum tests

Key Stage 2

Test 4

Mathematics

Paper 1: arithmetic

First name						
Middle name						
Last name						
Date of birth	Day		Month		Year	
School name						

Total Marks	/ 40

Instructions

You **may not** use a calculator to answer any questions in this test.

Questions and answers

You have **30 minutes** to complete this test.

Work as quickly and as carefully as you can.

Put your answer in the box for each question.

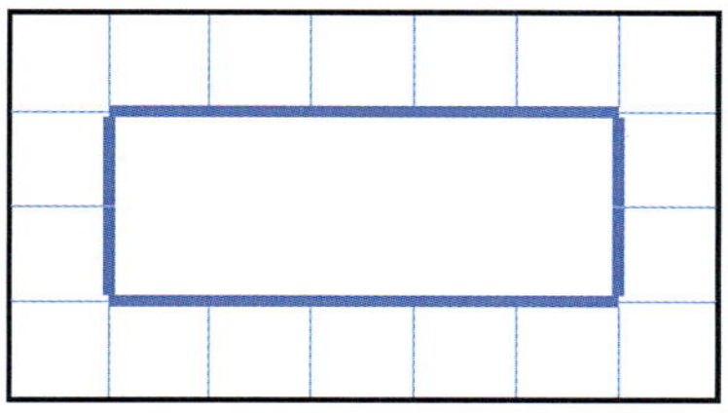

For questions expressed as common fractions, you should give your answers as common fractions.

All other answers should be given as either whole or decimal numbers.

If you cannot do one of the questions, **go on to the next one.** You can come back to it later if you have time.

If you finish before the end, **go back and check your work.**

Marks

The number under each box at the side of the page tells you the maximum number of marks for each question.

In this test, long division and long multiplication questions are worth **2 marks each.** You will be awarded 2 marks for a correct answer.

You may get 1 mark for showing a formal method.

All other questions are worth **1 mark each.**

If you finish before the end, go back and check your work.

1

5^2 =

1 mark

2

561 x 2 =

1 mark

3

1.2 + 6.1 =

1 mark

4

2 x 6 x 5 =

1 mark

5

35 x 4 =

1 mark

6

631 - 224 =

1 mark

7

238 - 10 =

1 mark

8

24 ÷ 6 =

1 mark

9

904 - 7 =

1 mark

10

$1.3 + 0.14 =$

1 mark

11

$\frac{1}{11} + \frac{5}{11} =$

1 mark

12

$0.31 \times 1{,}000 =$

1 mark

13

88 ÷ 8 =

1 mark

14

30,000 - 500 =

1 mark

15

300 x 100 =

1 mark

16

$242 \div 11 =$

1 mark

17

10% of 30 =

1 mark

18

$6.14 \times 3 =$

1 mark

19

9 - 1.77 =

1 mark

20

$\frac{1}{15} + \frac{8}{15} =$

1 mark

21

4,012 + 3,001 =

1 mark

22

$1{,}482 \div 6 =$

1 mark

23

$\frac{3}{5} + \frac{1}{12} =$

1 mark

24

$$\begin{array}{r} 35 \\ \times\ 41 \\ \hline \end{array}$$

Show your method

2 marks

25

13.8 - 0.15 =

1 mark

26

216 ÷ 6 =

1 mark

27

$23\overline{)2875}$

Show your method

2 marks

28

20% of 65 =

1 mark

29

412,784 + 31,451 =

1 mark

30

$12 \times 1\frac{2}{3} =$

1 mark

31

524,915 - 11,791 =

1 mark

32

$\frac{3}{8} \div 4 =$

1 mark

33

$3\frac{3}{4} - \frac{1}{2} =$

1 mark

34

$$52\overline{)1196}$$

Show your method

2 marks

35

$$\frac{2}{5} + \frac{1}{8} =$$

1 mark

36

$$\begin{array}{r} 145 \\ \times \quad 25 \\ \hline \end{array}$$

Show your method

2 marks

National curriculum tests

Key Stage 2

Test 1

Mathematics

Paper 2: reasoning

First name						
Middle name						
Last name						
Date of birth	Day		Month		Year	
School name						

Total Marks	/ 35

Instructions

You **may not** use a calculator to answer any questions in this test.

Questions and answers

You have **40 minutes** to complete this test.

Follow the instructions for each question.

Work as quickly and as carefully as you can.

If you need to do working out, you can use the space around the question.

Some questions have a method box like this:

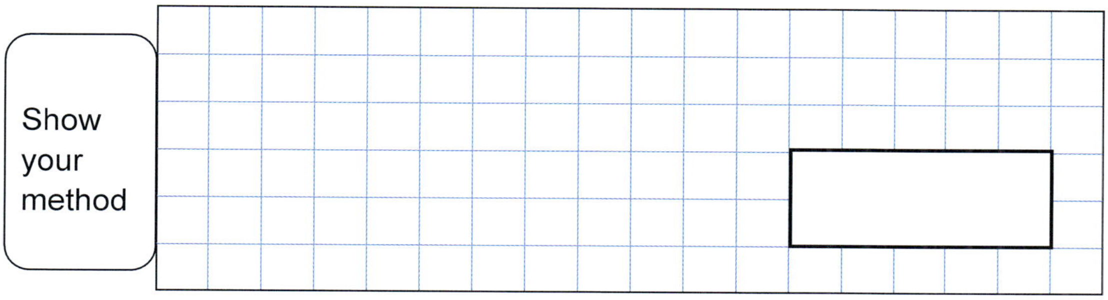

For these questions you may get a mark for showing your method.

If you cannot do one of the questions, **go on to the next one.** You can come back to it later, if you have time.

If you finish before the end, **go back and check your work.**

Marks

The number under each line at the side of the page tells you the maximum number of marks for each question.

1 Write the two missing numbers.

One is done for you.

202 —is 30 more than→ 172

[ ] —is 30 more than→ 152

[ ] —is 30 less than→ 152

1 mark

2 Here is a number written in Roman numerals.

DLIII

Write the number in figures.

[ ]

1 mark

3 Circle the number that is closest to 5000

5015 **5050** **5115** **4120**

1 mark

4 Identify each pair of shapes as a reflection or a translation.

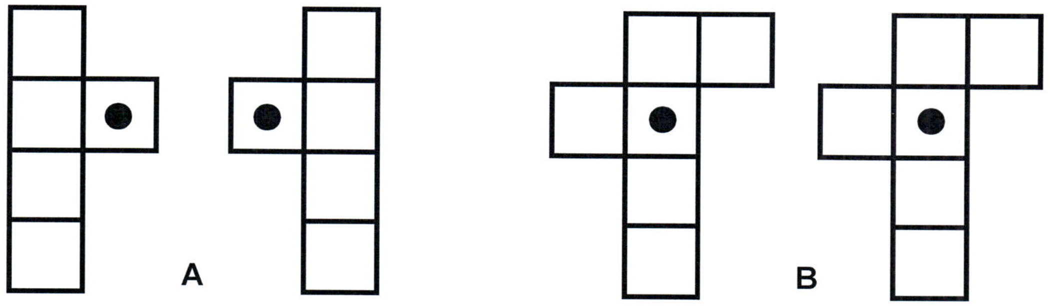

Translation = ☐ **Reflection** = ☐

2 marks

5 A parcel is 18 cm long, 12 cm wide and 10 cm high.

What is the volume of the parcel?

☐ **cm³**

2 marks

6 What is 461 minutes in hours and minutes?

☐ **hours** ☐ **minutes**

1 mark

7 Lucy collected 504 different stamps.

She made a collection of books with 36 stamps in each book.

How many books of stamps did Lucy make?

books

2 marks

8 Look at the diagram below. It shows an equilateral triangle inside a rectangle.

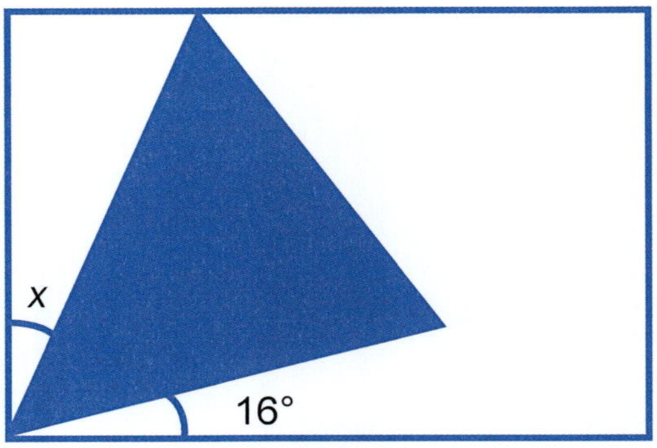

Calculate the size of angle *x*.

Show your method

x is °

2 marks

9 Match each fraction to its equivalent below.

$\frac{1}{2}$	$\frac{9}{21}$
$\frac{3}{7}$	$\frac{10}{16}$
$\frac{5}{8}$	$\frac{11}{22}$

2 marks

10 Write these fractions in order of size, starting with the smallest.

$\frac{2}{5}$ $\frac{5}{6}$ $\frac{8}{10}$ $\frac{3}{8}$ $\frac{4}{7}$

smallest

2 marks

11 The perimeter of this rectangle is 60 centimetres.

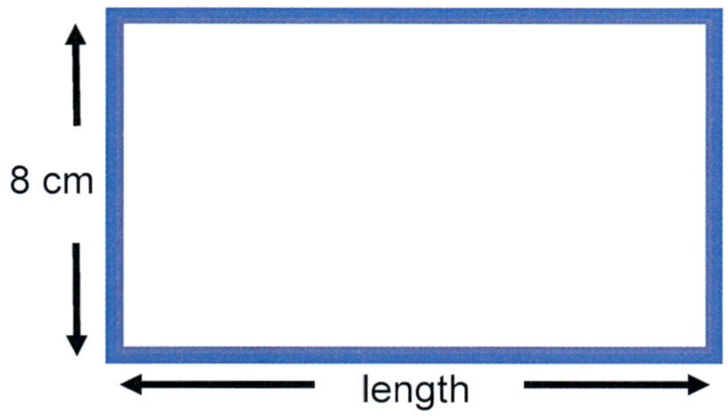

Not actual size

Calculate the length of the rectangle.

cm

2 marks

12 Two decimal numbers add together to equal 1

One of the numbers is 0.023

What is the other number?

1 mark

13 Here are the ingredients for a cake.

Cake ingredients:	
flour	200 grams
butter	140 grams
sugar	200 grams

Lucy has only 105 grams of butter to make a cake.

How much flour should she use?

Show your method

grams

2 marks

14 Here is an equation.

$m - 2n = 22$

(a) When $n = 40$ what is the value of m?

$m =$

1 mark

(b) When $m = 40$ what is the value of n?

$n =$

1 mark

15 Find the area of this parallelogram.

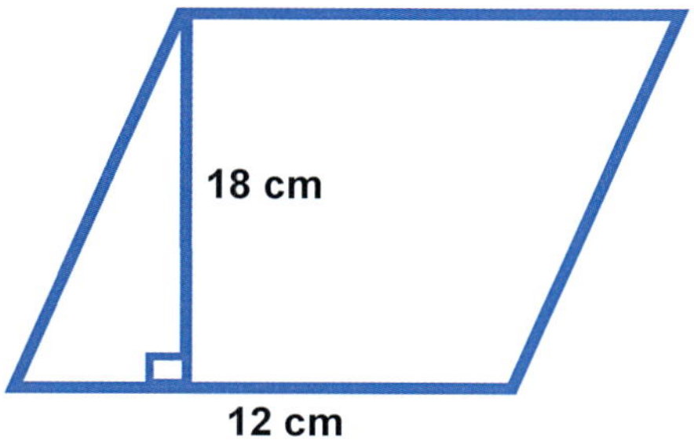

cm^2

2 marks

16 Complete the descriptions of the 3-D shapes below.

Shape	Number of faces	Number of vertices	Number of edges
Triangular pyramid			
Square pyramid			

2 marks

17 Calculate the diameter.

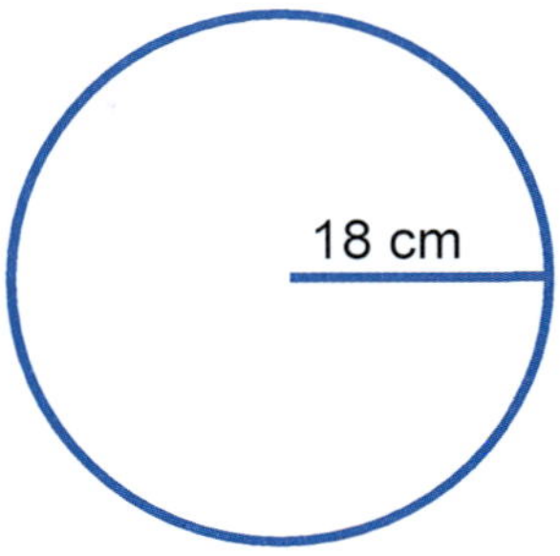

cm

2 marks

18 Calculate the size of angle *x*.

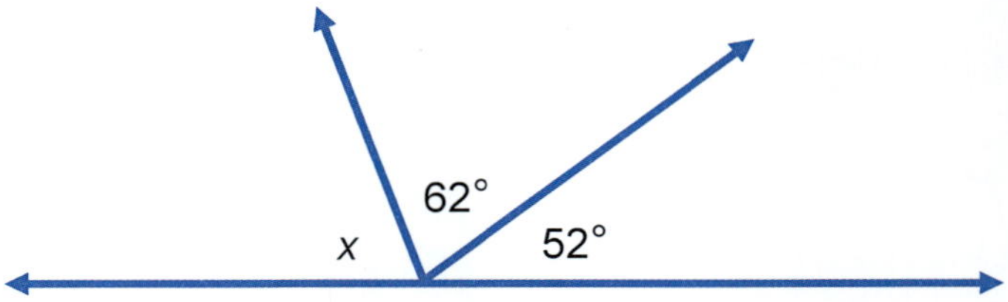

Show your method

x is °

2 marks

19 Five pupils achieved the following results in a class test.

Jack	Chloe	Michael	Lucy	Anika
15	12	15	13	10

What was the mean result achieved in the test?

Show your method

2 marks

20 In Miss Brown's class, one in every 6 pupils wears glasses.

There are 42 pupils in the class.

How many pupils do not wear glasses?

Show your method

pupils

2 marks

National curriculum tests

Key Stage 2

Test 2

Mathematics

Paper 2: reasoning

First name						
Middle name						
Last name						
Date of birth	Day		Month		Year	
School name						

Total Marks	/ 35

Instructions

You **may not** use a calculator to answer any questions in this test.

Questions and answers

You have **40 minutes** to complete this test.

Follow the instructions for each question.

Work as quickly and as carefully as you can.

If you need to do working out, you can use the space around the question.

Some questions have a method box like this:

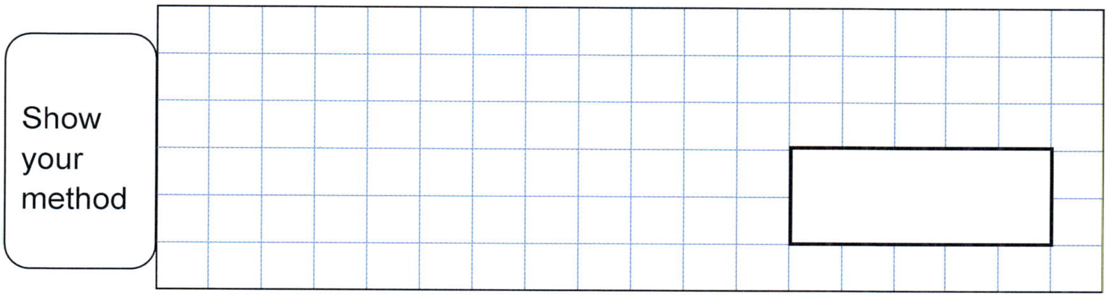

For these questions you may get a mark for showing your method.

If you cannot do one of the questions, **go on to the next one.** You can come back to it later, if you have time.

If you finish before the end, **go back and check your work.**

Marks

The number under each line at the side of the page tells you the maximum number of marks for each question.

1 Look at this number.

4250.38

Write the digit that is in the thousands place.

[ ]

1 mark

2 Jack thinks of a number less than 50

He adds 4 and then multiplies the number by 11

His answer is 132

What was the number he started with?

[ ]

1 mark

3 A box can hold 338 eggs.

If there are 26 rows in a box, how many columns are there?

Show your method

[ ] **columns**

2 marks

4 The radius of a circle is 4.25 cm.

What is the diameter?

| cm |

1 mark

5 Find the mean mass of three parcels weighing 4 kg, 3 kg and 14 kg.

Show your method

| kg |

2 marks

6 Write all of the factor pairs for the number 12

(,) (,) (,)

2 marks

7 Match each fraction to its equivalent below.

$\frac{4}{5}$	$\frac{18}{30}$
$\frac{1}{9}$	$\frac{20}{25}$
$\frac{3}{5}$	$\frac{6}{54}$

2 marks

8 A box contains 80 matches and weighs 22 grams.

The empty box weighs 6 grams.

Calculate the weight of one match.

Show your method

grams

2 marks

9 $4 + x = 9x$

What is the value of x in this equation?

$x =$

2 marks

10 James achieved the following marks in two of his school tests.

Maths	Science
19 marks out of 35	23 marks out of 45

Which subject did he perform better in?

____

2 marks

11 Write these fractions in order of size, starting with the smallest.

$\frac{2}{5}$ $\frac{4}{10}$ $\frac{11}{15}$ $\frac{7}{9}$ $\frac{2}{8}$

☐ ☐ ☐ ☐ ☐

smallest

2 marks

12 Look at these equations.

$a + b + c = 24$

$b - c = 4$

$a + b = 16$

What is the value of *a*, *b* and *c*?

$a =$ ☐ $b =$ ☐ $c =$ ☐

2 marks

13 Complete the descriptions of the 3-D shapes below.

Shape	Number of faces	Number of vertices	Number of edges
Triangular prism			
Rectangular prism			

2 marks

14 ABCD is a rectangle drawn on coordinate axes.

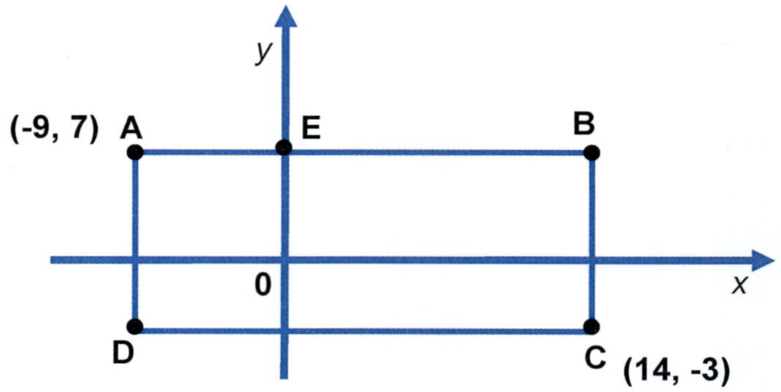

Not to scale

What are the coordinates of D and E?

D = (,   )

1 mark

E = (,   )

1 mark

15 Mary walks one and a quarter miles to school each day.

1 mile = 1.6 kilometres

Using the conversion table above, how many kilometres does she walk each day?

km

2 marks

16 **a)** Lucy makes badges and sells them in boxes. She uses this formula to work how much to charge for one box of badges.

Cost = number of badges x 15p + £1.15 for the box

How much will a box of 14 badges cost?

£

1 mark

b) Michael buys a box of badges for £4.15

Use the formula to calculate how many badges are in his box.

Show your method

badges

2 marks

17 This bar graph shows how much Anika raised each month for her local charity.

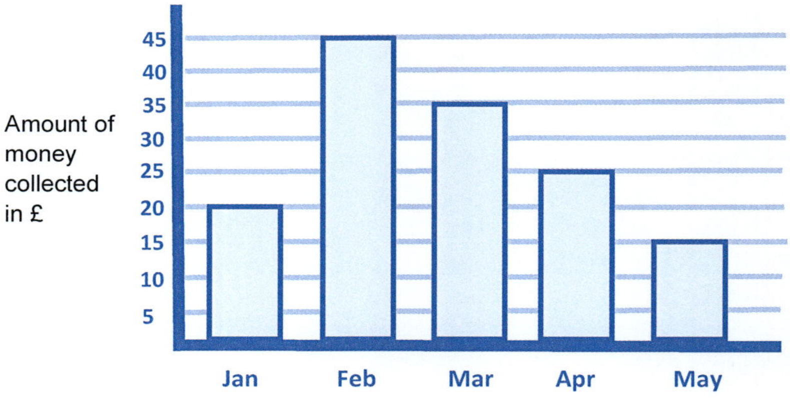

a) How much money did she raise in April and May altogether?

£

1 mark

b) How much money had she raised by the end of March?

£

1 mark

18 Here is a number written in Roman numerals.

DCCCXLI

Write the number in figures.

1 mark

19 Jack leaves school at 3.45 pm.

His sister, Chloe, leaves school 24 minutes later.

The journey home takes approximately 32 minutes.

At what time will each of them arrive home?

Jack:

1 mark

Chloe:

1 mark

National curriculum tests

Key Stage 2

Test 3

Mathematics

Paper 2: reasoning

First name						
Middle name						
Last name						
Date of birth	Day		Month		Year	
School name						

Total Marks	/ 35

Instructions

You **may not** use a calculator to answer any questions in this test.

Questions and answers

You have **40 minutes** to complete this test.

Follow the instructions for each question.

Work as quickly and as carefully as you can.

If you need to do working out, you can use the space around the question.

Some questions have a method box like this:

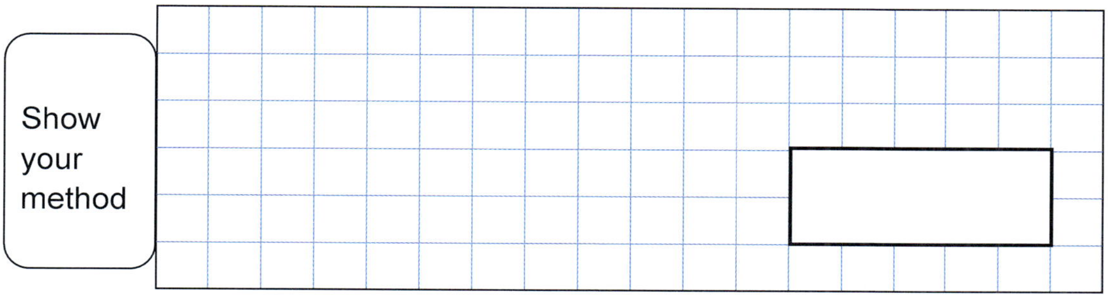

For these questions you may get a mark for showing your method.

If you cannot do one of the questions, **go on to the next one.** You can come back to it later, if you have time.

If you finish before the end, **go back and check your work.**

Marks

The number under each line at the side of the page tells you the maximum number of marks for each question.

1 Below is part of a number line.

Write the missing numbers in the boxes.

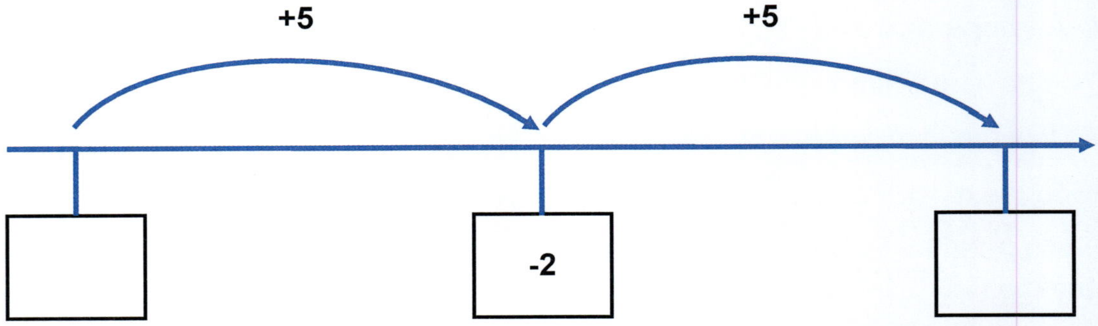

2 marks

2 Write all the common factors of 20 and 30

____

1 mark

3 Identify each pair of shapes as a reflection or a translation.

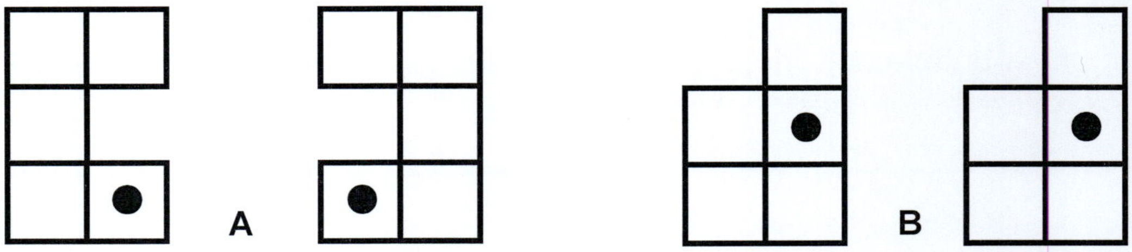

Translation = ☐ **Reflection** = ☐

2 marks

4 Write the missing numbers.

One is done for you.

326	is 40 more than →	286
☐	is 40 more than →	463
☐	is 40 less than →	463

1 mark

5 Paper clips are sold in packs of 36

Claire needs 450 paper clips.

How many packs must she buy?

☐ **packs**

2 marks

6 Round **184,421**

to the nearest 10,000 ☐

to the nearest 1,000 ☐

to the nearest 100 ☐

2 marks

7 Write these fractions in order of size, starting with the smallest.

$\frac{3}{4}$ $\frac{7}{10}$ $\frac{11}{12}$ $\frac{4}{7}$ $\frac{2}{9}$

smallest				

2 marks

8 Find the area and perimeter of the shape below.

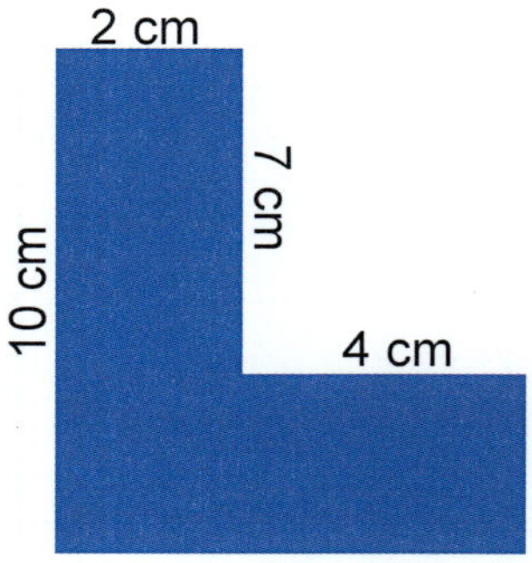

Area = $\square$ **cm²**

1 mark

Perimeter = $\square$ **cm**

1 mark

9 Lucy buys 12 boxes of eggs for £15.12

Each box contains 6 eggs.

What is the price of 1 egg?

£ $\square$

2 marks

10 Convert the fraction below to its decimal equivalent.

Fraction	Decimal
$\frac{4}{10}$	

1 mark

11 List all the prime numbers between 40 and 50

____

2 marks

12 One gram of gold costs £8.57

What is the cost of half a kilogram of gold?

£

2 marks

13 What is half of $\frac{5}{8}$?

2 marks

14 Here is a number written in Roman numerals.

XXXIV

Write the number in figures.

1 mark

15 Which 3-D shape is described below?

"This shape has 1 face which is a circle. It has one curved surface area. It has no edges or vertices."

2 marks

16 Draw a line to show which angle is acute, obtuse or reflex.

A

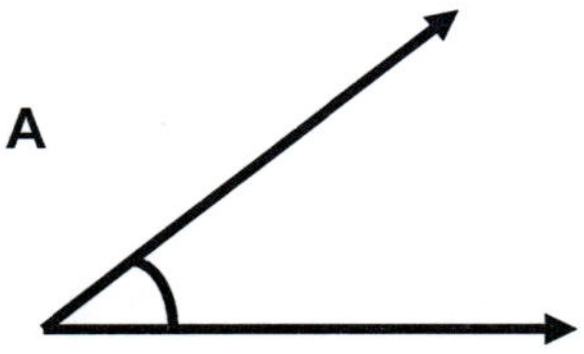

Reflex

B

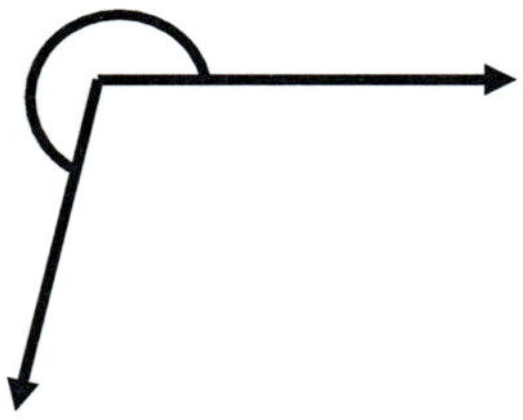

Acute

C

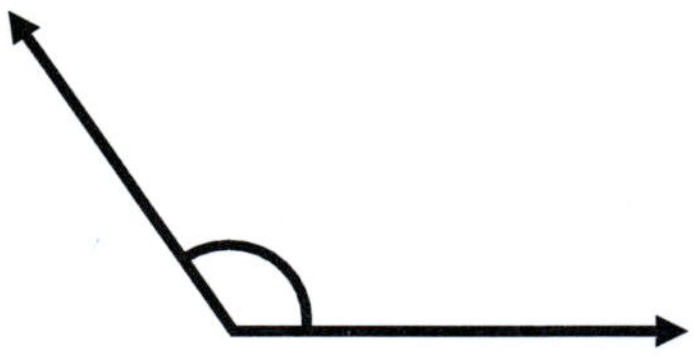

Obtuse

2 marks

17 Calculate the diameter.

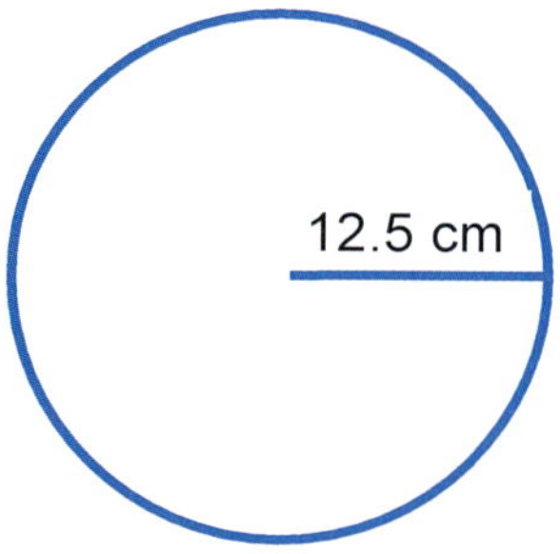

cm

2 marks

18 On Thursday Jack painted his room and used $\frac{2}{5}$ of a tin of paint.

On Friday he finished painting his room and used the remaining 285 ml.

How many ml of paint did Jack use to paint his room?

Show your method

ml

2 marks

19 What number is half way between 0.5 and 1.6?

1 mark

20 Calculate the size of angle R.

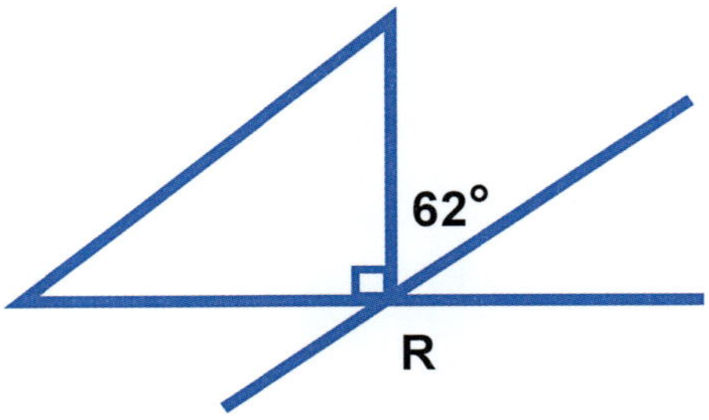

Show your method

R = °

2 marks

National curriculum tests

Key Stage 2

Test 4

Mathematics

Paper 2: reasoning

First name						
Middle name						
Last name						
Date of birth	Day		Month		Year	
School name						

Total Marks	/ 35

Instructions

You **may not** use a calculator to answer any questions in this test.

Questions and answers

You have **40 minutes** to complete this test.

Follow the instructions for each question.

Work as quickly and as carefully as you can.

If you need to do working out, you can use the space around the question.

Some questions have a method box like this:

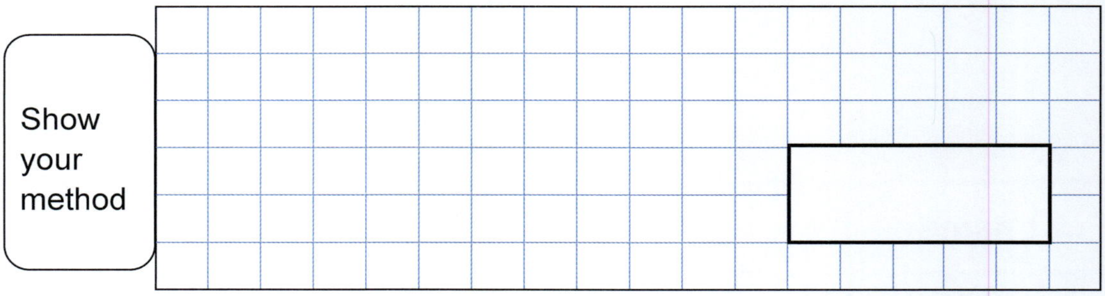

For these questions you may get a mark for showing your method.

If you cannot do one of the questions, **go on to the next one.** You can come back to it later, if you have time.

If you finish before the end, **go back and check your work.**

Marks

The number under each line at the side of the page tells you the maximum number of marks for each question.

1 Look at this number.

23,847.51

Write the digit that is in the hundredths place.

[ ]

1 mark

2 One side of a regular hexagon measures 4.5 cm.

What is the perimeter of the shape?

[ ] **cm**

2 marks

3 Lucy makes a sequence of numbers starting with 1

She subtracts 11 each time.

Write the next 2 numbers in Lucy's sequence.

[ ] [ ]

2 marks

4 Joseph's watch shows seven minutes past 6

The watch is eleven minutes fast.

What is the correct time?

[ ]

1 mark

5 Write the missing numbers.

One is done for you.

8,951	is 60 more than →	8,891
[ ]	is 60 more than →	1,999
[ ]	is 60 less than →	1,999

1 mark

6 On a 1.32 scale model of a school, the playground is 3 cm wide.

How wide is the actual playground in metres?

Show your method

[ ] **metres**

2 marks

7 Lisa spends £23.22 and Gemma spends £42.96 at their local shop.

How much more money does Gemma spend than Lisa?

Show your method

£

2 marks

8 Calculate the size of angle *x*.

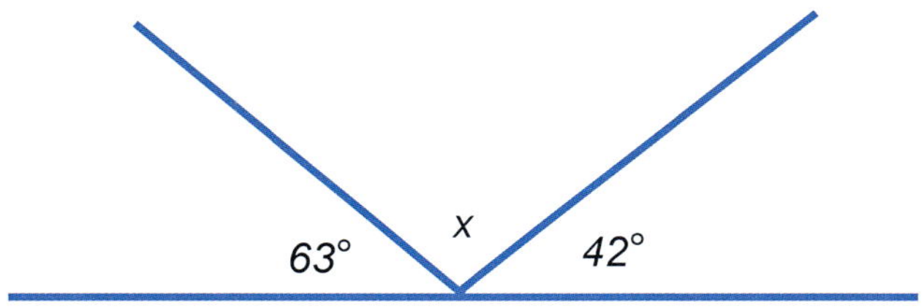

x is °

2 marks

9 Identify the numbers which are **not** factors of 40

10 **14** **20** **24** **40**

____

1 mark

10 Claire has 8 kilograms of flour.

She mixes 6 kilograms of flour with 1 litre of water.

What percentage of flour does she have left?

[ ] %

2 marks

11 Write the missing number.

$\square \div 2.5 = 6.5 \div 1.3$

1 mark

12 One kilogram of sugar costs £1.08

What is the cost of 250 grams of sugar?

Show your method

£ [ ]

2 marks

13 Here is a recipe for fresh lemonade.

Lemon juice	30 ml
Water	400 ml
Sugar	30 g

Alex has only 24 g of sugar.

How much water should he use?

Show your method

ml

2 marks

14 $3 + n = 13n$

What is the value of n in this equation?

$n =$

2 marks

15 Find the area of this triangle.

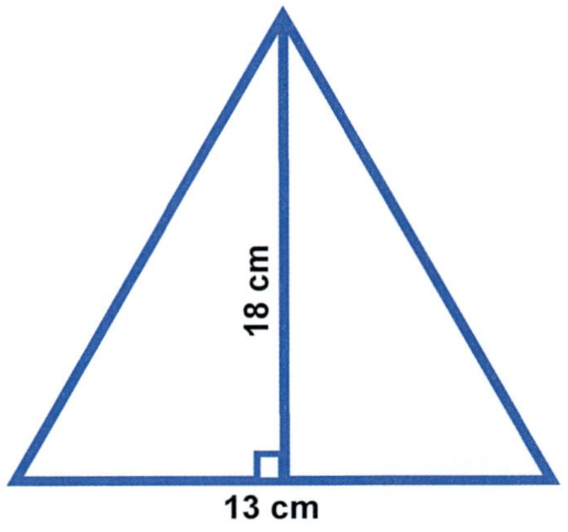

cm²

2 marks

16 Round 793,201

to the nearest 10,000

to the nearest 1,000

to the nearest 100

2 marks

17 Mrs Smith ordered 168 exercise books for her class of 24 pupils.

How many exercise books will each pupil receive?

Show your method

books

2 marks

18 What percentage of 56 is 42?

Show your method

%

2 marks

19 The diameter of a circle is 12.5 cm.

What is the radius?

cm

2 marks

20 Convert 5.068 kilograms to grams.

grams

2 marks

National curriculum tests

Key Stage 2

Test 1

Mathematics

Paper 3: reasoning

First name						
Middle name						
Last name						
Date of birth	Day		Month		Year	
School name						

Total Marks	/ 35

Reasoning: Paper 3, Test 1

Instructions

You **may not** use a calculator to answer any questions in this test.

Questions and answers

You have **40 minutes** to complete this test.

Follow the instructions for each question.

Work as quickly and as carefully as you can.

If you need to do working out, you can use the space around the question.

Some questions have a method box like this:

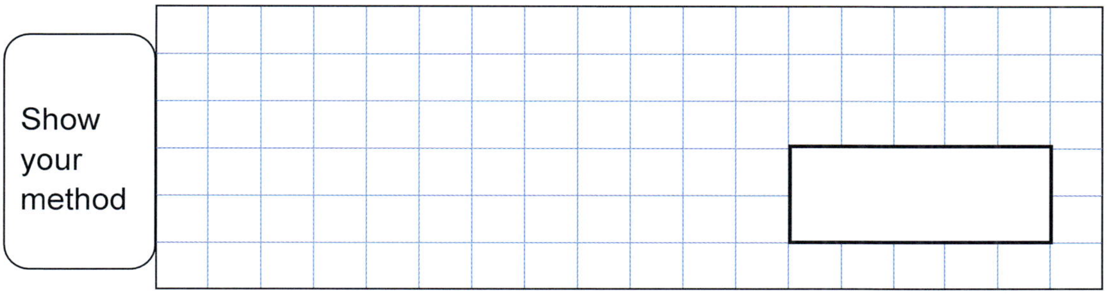

For these questions you may get a mark for showing your method.

If you cannot do one of the questions, **go on to the next one.** You can come back to it later, if you have time.

If you finish before the end, **go back and check your work.**

Marks

The number under each line at the side of the page tells you the maximum number of marks for each question.

1 The numbers in this sequence increase by the same amount each time.

Write the two missing numbers.

	645,612	**648,612**	**651,612**	

1 mark

2 A box of crayons has 135 crayons.

6 pupils each take 7 crayons.

How many crayons are left in the box?

Show your method

crayons

1 mark

3 Chloe thinks of a number less than 50. She multiplies the number by itself and then adds 18

Her answer is 54

What was the number she started with?

1 mark

4 Look at this number.

413,785.26

Write the digit that is in the hundredths place.

[ ]

1 mark

5 Jack buys 8 chocolate bars and 12 packets of crisps.

Chocolate bar	Packet of crisps
£0.74	£0.62

How much does he pay for the items altogether?

£ [ ]

1 mark

6 Complete the following table.

Decimal	Fraction	Percentage
	$\frac{2}{5}$	

2 marks

7 This model is made with 8 cubes.

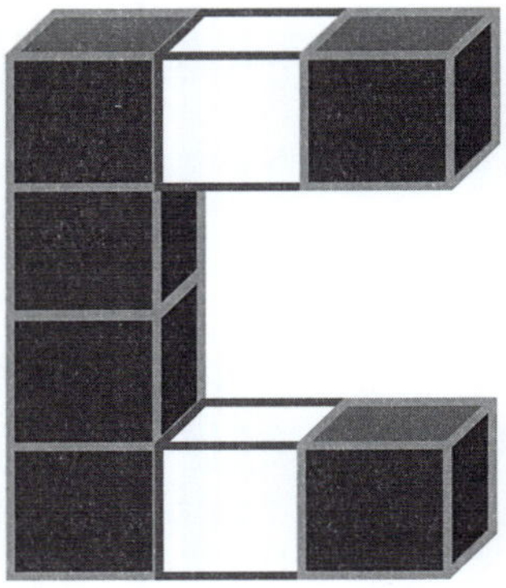

What percentage of the cubes in the model is black?

| %

2 marks

8 Identify all of the composite numbers below.

6	13	17	19	20	27

____

1 mark

9 Put a tick in each box to show which shape is a regular or irregular polygon.

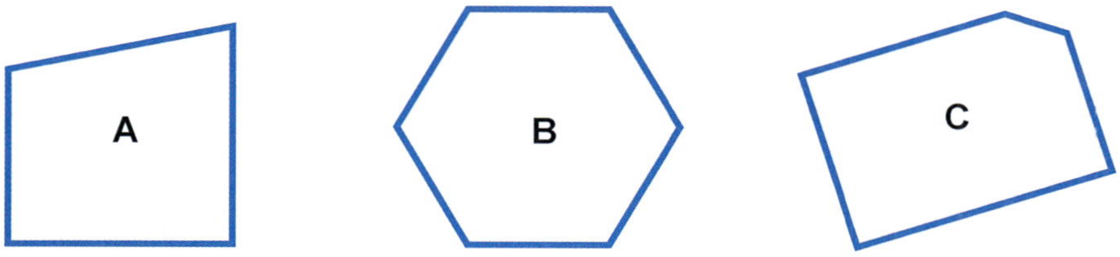

	Regular polygon	Irregular polygon
A		
B		
C		

2 marks

10 In this equation n stands for a number.

$$6n - 3 = 3n + 6$$

What is the value of n?

Show your method

$n =$

2 marks

11 Identify all the multiples of 7

3,402	4,417	3,625	4,424	4,621

____

2 marks

12 One side of a regular octagon measures 7.5 cm

What is the perimeter of the shape?

[ ] cm

2 marks

13 Draw a line to show which angle is acute, obtuse or reflex.

A
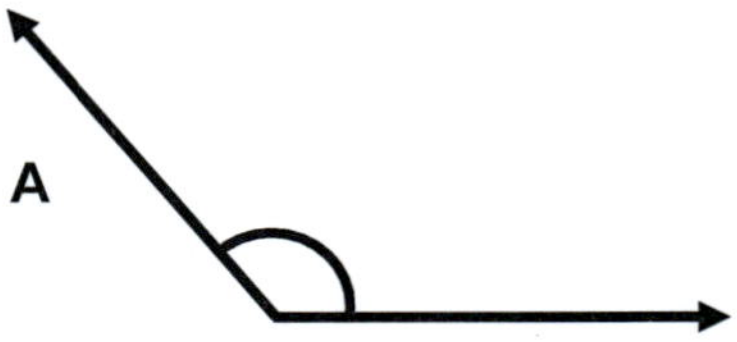

B
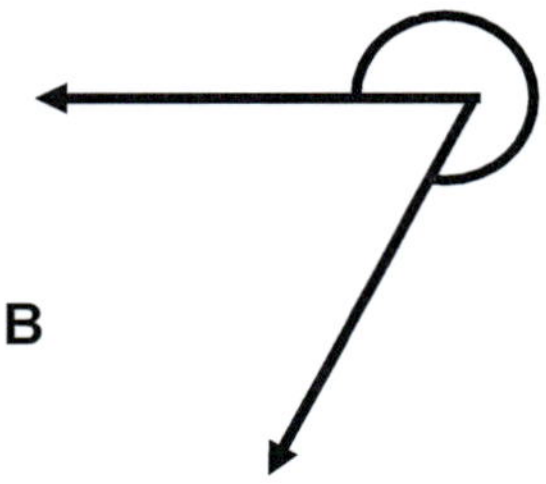

C
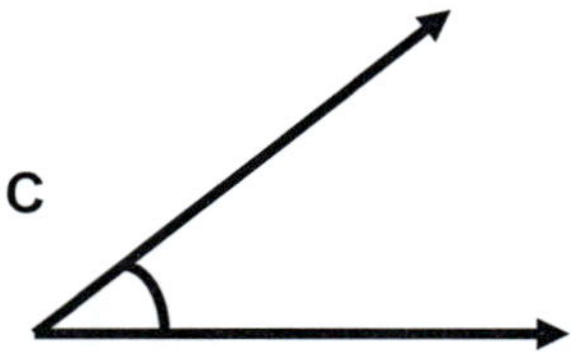

Reflex

Acute

Obtuse

2 marks

14 Write 8050 centimetres in metres.

____

1 mark

15 If B is the midpoint of AC, find the coordinate of C.

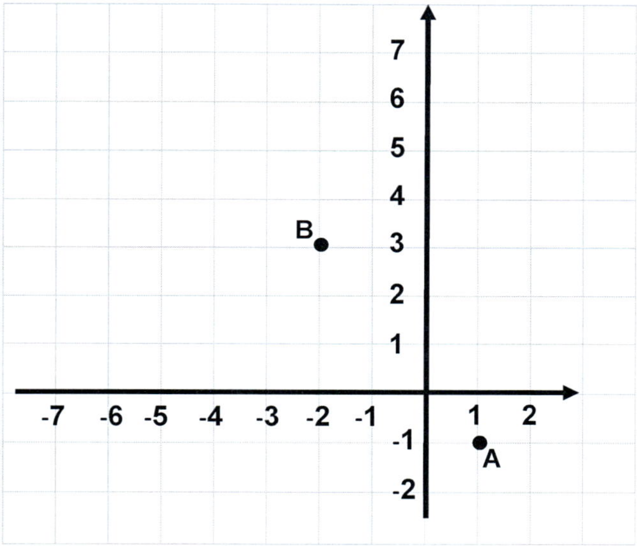

(,)

2 marks

16 Complete the table below.

Analogue	Digital
7:35 pm	
1:02 pm	
12:06 am	

2 marks

17 Identify the following 3-D shape.

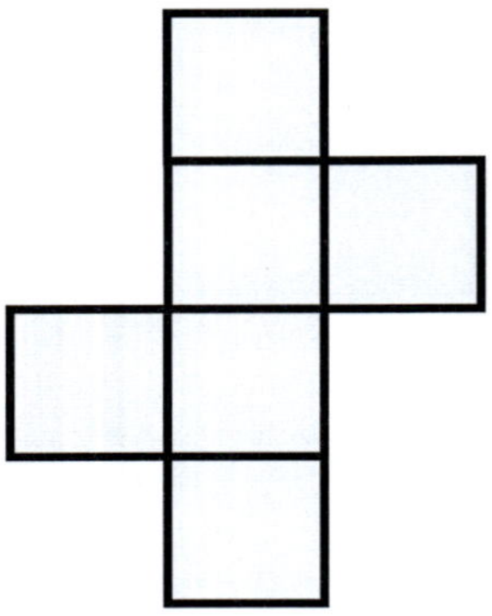

____

2 marks

18 Find the area of this triangle.

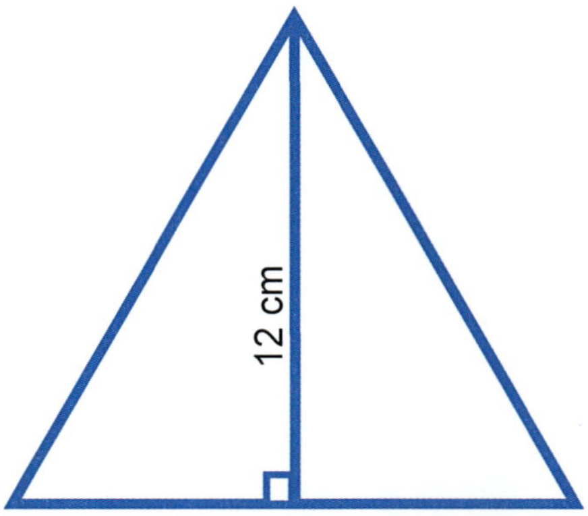

Show your method

cm²

2 marks

19 Complete the table below.

Shape	Number of lines of symmetry
Rectangle	
Isosceles triangle	
Regular hexagon	

2 marks

20 Identify each part of the circle.

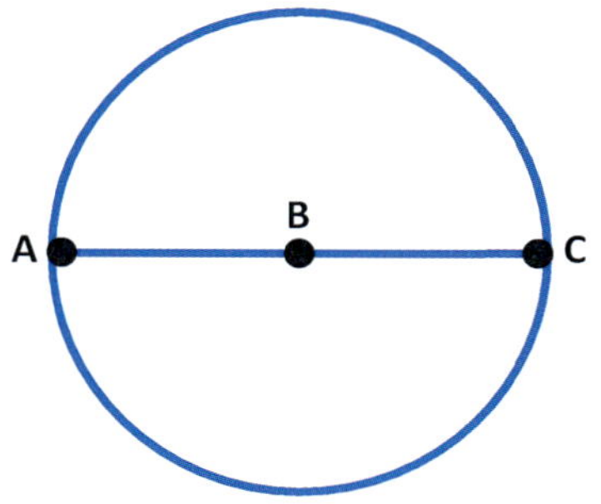

AC = ______ BA, BC = ______

2 marks

21 On a 1:500 scale model of a house, the chimney is 8 centimetres tall.

How tall is the actual chimney in metres?

Show your method

______ metres

2 marks

National curriculum tests

Key Stage 2

Test 2

Mathematics

Paper 3: reasoning

First name						
Middle name						
Last name						
Date of birth	Day		Month		Year	
School name						

Total Marks	/ 35

Instructions

You **may not** use a calculator to answer any questions in this test.

Questions and answers

You have **40 minutes** to complete this test.

Follow the instructions for each question.

Work as quickly and as carefully as you can.

If you need to do working out, you can use the space around the question.

Some questions have a method box like this:

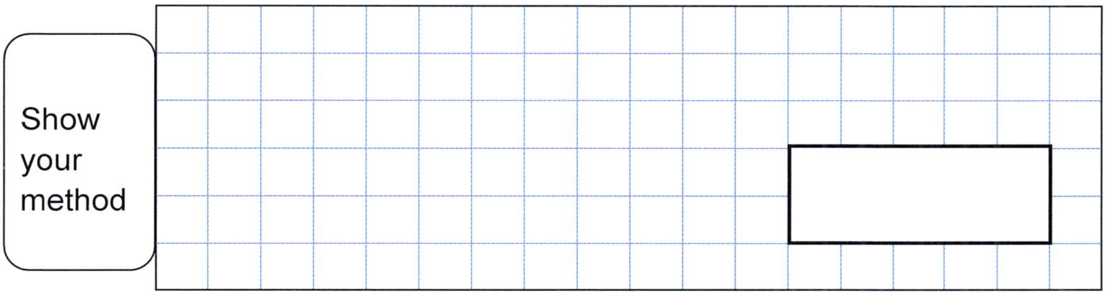

For these questions you may get a mark for showing your method.

If you cannot do one of the questions, **go on to the next one.** You can come back to it later, if you have time.

If you finish before the end, **go back and check your work.**

Marks

The number under each line at the side of the page tells you the maximum number of marks for each question.

1 What is 4:32 pm in 24-hour time?

1 mark

2 James has 840 ml of lemonade.

How many 140 ml glasses can he fill?

glasses

1 mark

3 Complete each calculation below.

5.2 ÷ 10 =

5.2 x 100 =

5.2 ÷ 100 =

2 marks

4 Classify each angle as acute, obtuse or reflex.

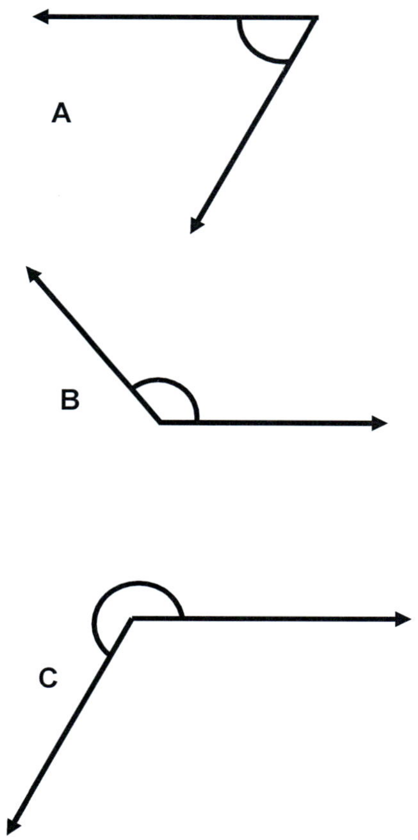

Reflex

Acute

Obtuse

2 marks

5 Complete the table below.

Decimal	Fraction	Percentage
	$\frac{4}{5}$	

2 marks

6 What is one half multiplied by one third?

2 marks

7 Identify the following 3-D shape.

2 marks

8 Sort these decimals in order of size, starting with the smallest.

423.60 423.186 423.116 423.06 423.16

smallest

2 marks

9 Look at this number.

468,572.31

Write the digit that is in the hundredths place.

1 mark

10 Find the area of this parallelogram.

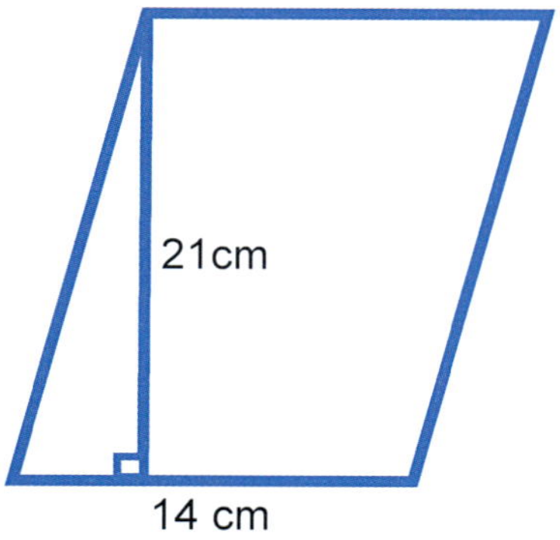

Show your method

cm²

2 marks

11 The radius of a circle is 6.5 cm.

What is the diameter?

cm

2 marks

12 What number is halfway between 4.1 and 1.5?

1 mark

13 The numbers in this sequence increase by the same amount each time.

Write the two missing numbers.

	218,924	**219,224**		**219,824**

1 mark

14 **4*a* + 8 = 20**

Solve this calculation.

Show your method

a **=**

2 marks

15 Here is a rectangle on coordinate axes.

Find the coordinates of B and D.

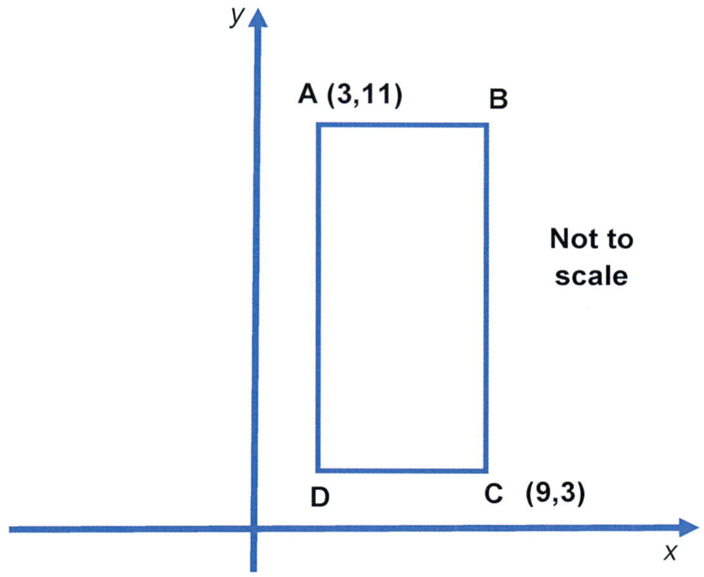

B = (,)

1 mark

D = (,)

1 mark

16 Identify all the common multiples of the numbers 9 and 25

225	325	450	525	675

____

2 marks

17 Five pupils take part in a race.

Their following times were recorded.

Pupil A	Pupil B	Pupil C	Pupil D	Pupil E
18 seconds	26 seconds	19 seconds	17 seconds	15 seconds

What was the mean time achieved in the race?

Show your method

seconds

2 marks

18 A basketball costs £3.22 more than a football.

Jack buys two footballs and one basketball for £16.06

How much does a football cost?

Show your method

£

2 marks

19 Complete the table below.

Shape	Number of lines of symmetry
Square	
Rhombus	
Equilateral triangle	

2 marks

20 Michael builds a cuboid using 64 centimetre cubes.

His cuboid is 8 cm long and 4 cm wide.

Calculate the height of the cuboid.

Show your method

cm

2 marks

National curriculum tests

Key Stage 2

Test 3

Mathematics

Paper 3: reasoning

First name						
Middle name						
Last name						
Date of birth	Day		Month		Year	
School name						

Total Marks	/ 35

Instructions

You **may not** use a calculator to answer any questions in this test.

Questions and answers

You have **40 minutes** to complete this test.

Follow the instructions for each question.

Work as quickly and as carefully as you can.

If you need to do working out, you can use the space around the question.

Some questions have a method box like this:

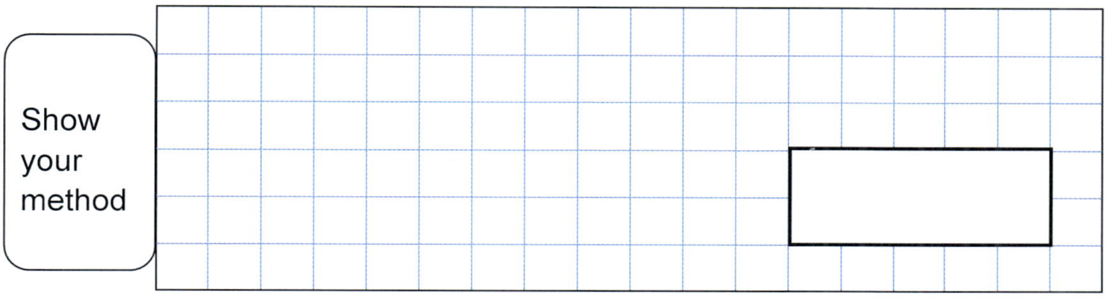

For these questions you may get a mark for showing your method.

If you cannot do one of the questions, **go on to the next one.** You can come back to it later, if you have time.

If you finish before the end, **go back and check your work.**

Marks

The number under each line at the side of the page tells you the maximum number of marks for each question.

1 Lisa spends £12.26 on food at the shop.

How much change will she receive from £20?

£

2 marks

2 What is £462.51 in pence?

pence

1 mark

3 Claire makes 1.6 litres of fresh orange juice.

She plans to sell glasses of juice measuring 200 ml.

How many glasses of juice can she make?

glasses

2 marks

4 Identify all the common multiples of the numbers 3 and 11

132	230	198	165	174

2 marks

5 25% of Lucy's number is 20

What is 35% of Lucy's number?

Show your method

2 marks

6 Match each fraction to its equivalent below.

$\frac{3}{4}$	$\frac{8}{20}$
$\frac{1}{6}$	$\frac{24}{32}$
$\frac{2}{5}$	$\frac{4}{24}$

2 marks

7 Round the number below to one decimal place.

2.16298

1 mark

8 Michael thinks of a number less than 200. He divides it by 2 and subtracts 12

He then divides this result by 2

His answer is 32

What was the number Michael started with?

2 marks

9 Write the missing numbers.

One is done for you.

1,281 —is 25 more than→ 1,256

[ ] —is 25 more than→ 2,516

[ ] —is 25 less than→ 2,516

1 mark

10 Calculate the size of angle *x*.

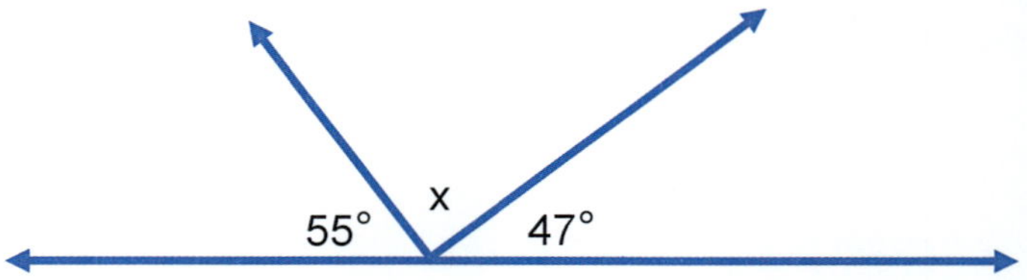

x is °

2 marks

11 What number is halfway between 1.2 and 3.6?

[ ]

1 mark

12 What is 429 minutes in hours and minutes?

[ ] **hours** [ ] **minutes**

1 mark

13 Gemma makes a cake and places it in the oven at 4.40 pm.

The cake needs to bake for 1 hour and 35 minutes.

At what time should Gemma take her cake out of the oven?

Show your method

[ ] **pm**

2 marks

14 Identify all of the factor pairs for the number 20

(,) (,) (,)

2 marks

15 Chloe makes a sequence of numbers starting with 2

She subtracts 5 each time.

Write the next 2 numbers in Chloe's sequence.

____

2 marks

16 Cheese costs £2.27 for 250 grams.

Claire buys 1 kilogram of cheese.

How much does Claire's cheese cost?

Show your method

£

2 marks

17 $8x - 5 = 1$

Calculate the value of x in this equation.

Show your method

$x =$

2 marks

18 Calculate the area of the shaded region.

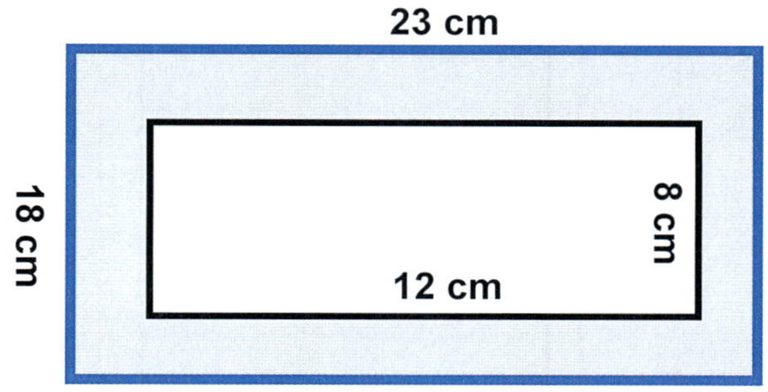

Show your method

cm^2

2 marks

19 ABCD is a square.

What are the coordinates of A and B?

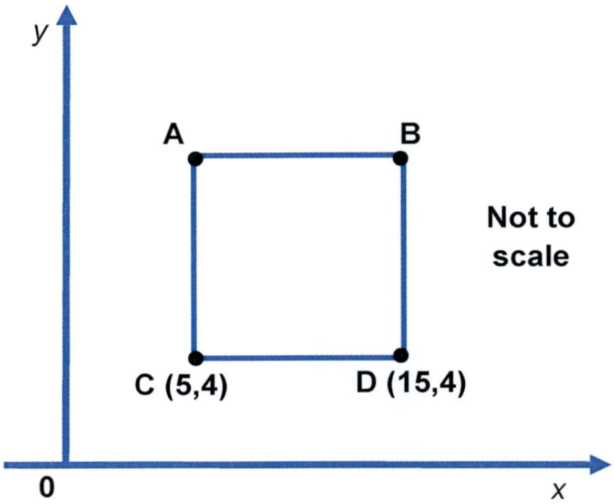

A = (,)

1 mark

B = (,)

1 mark

20 Identify the letter which points to six hundred thousand on the scale.

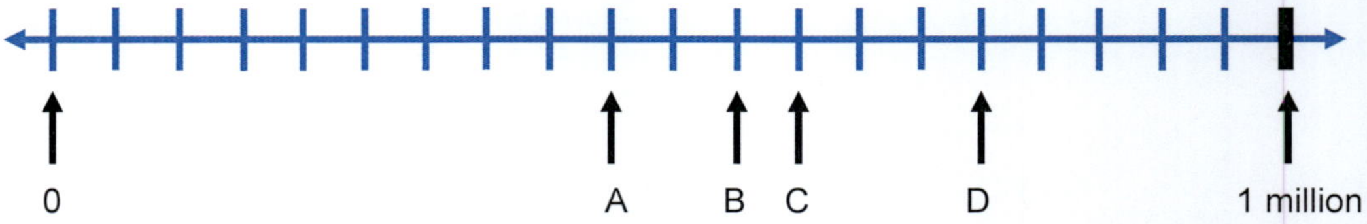

2 marks

National curriculum tests

Key Stage 2

Test 4

Mathematics

Paper 3: reasoning

First name					
Middle name					
Last name					
Date of birth	Day		Month		Year
School name					

Total Marks	/ 35

Reasoning: Paper 3, Test 4

Instructions

You **may not** use a calculator to answer any questions in this test.

Questions and answers

You have **40 minutes** to complete this test.

Follow the instructions for each question.

Work as quickly and as carefully as you can.

If you need to do working out, you can use the space around the question.

Some questions have a method box like this:

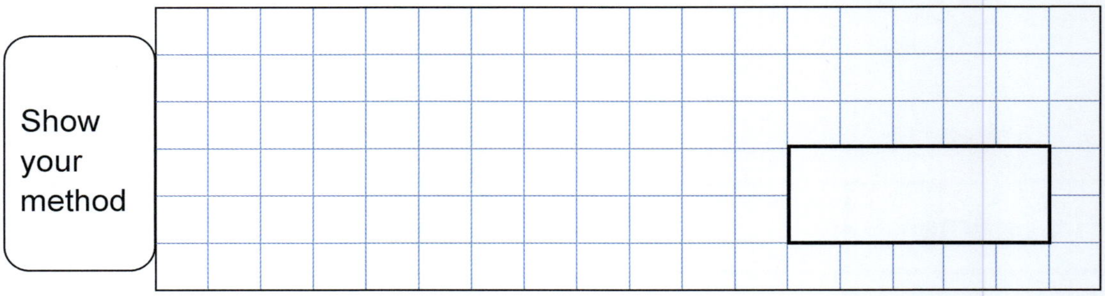

For these questions you may get a mark for showing your method.

If you cannot do one of the questions, **go on to the next one.** You can come back to it later, if you have time.

If you finish before the end, **go back and check your work.**

Marks

The number under each line at the side of the page tells you the maximum number of marks for each question.

1 Convert 22 grams to kilograms.

[   ] kg

1 mark

2 Simon thinks of a number less than 100

He divides it by 4 and adds 23

He then divides the number by 2

His answer is 19

What was the number he started with?

____

2 marks

3 Complete the table below.

Shape	Number of lines of symmetry
Square	
Rhombus	
Equilateral triangle	

2 marks

4 What is 281 minutes in hours and minutes?

hours	**minutes**

1 mark

5 The numbers in this sequence increase by the same amount each time.

Write the two missing numbers.

	294		**312**	**321**

1 mark

6 Calculate the area of the triangle below.

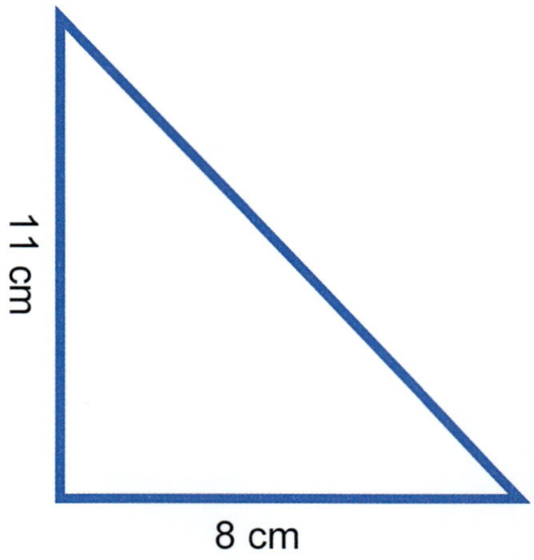

Show your method

cm²

2 marks

7 Complete the table below.

Decimal	Fraction	Percentage
	$\frac{1}{4}$	

1 mark

8 Calculate the volume of a crate measuring 14 cm long, 16 cm wide and 10 cm high.

cm^3

2 marks

9 How many 250 ml cups can be filled from a 2 litre bottle?

cups

2 marks

10 What is 75% of a quarter?

1 mark

11 Calculate the perimeter of the shape below.

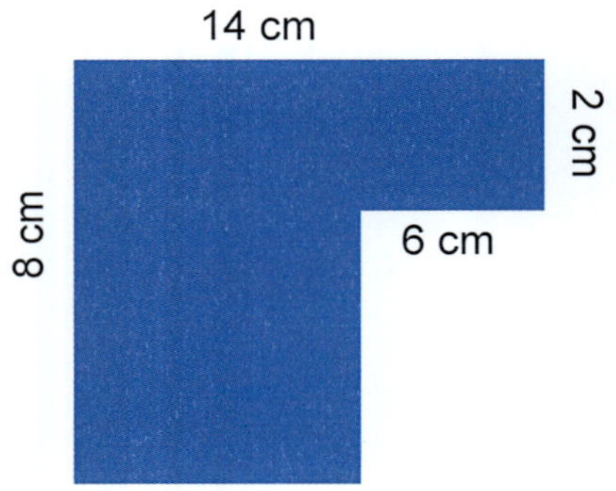

Show your method

cm

2 marks

12 Complete the descriptions of the 3-D shapes below.

Shape	Number of faces	Number of vertices	Number of edges
Triangular pyramid			
Triangular prism			

2 marks

13 Calculate the size of the missing angles in this parallelogram.

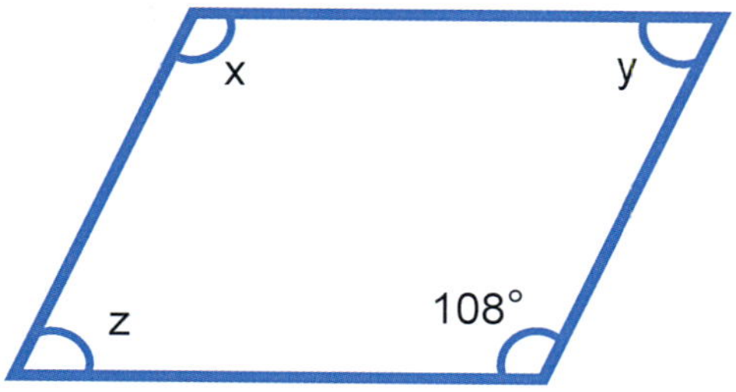

x = ° *y* = ° *z* = °

2 marks

14 Identify all the common multiples of 4 and 12

108	**146**	**168**	**180**	**194**

2 marks

15 Jack has £3,215 in his savings account.

He earns 6% interest on this amount.

How much will Jack have in his savings account after the interest has been added?

Show your method

£

2 marks

16 The diameter of a circle is 36 cm.

Calculate the radius.

cm

2 marks

17 Here is a number written in Roman numerals.

DCLXV

Write the number in figures.

1 mark

18 Lisa's birthday is on 3rd July. She held a birthday party 8 days before this date.

On what date did Lisa have her party?

____

1 mark

19 A teacher is organising transport for a school trip to the museum.

There are 236 pupils and 28 teachers going on the trip and each bus can hold 68 passengers.

How many buses will the teacher need to hire?

Show your method

buses

2 marks

20 One side of a regular hexagon measures 12 cm.

What is the perimeter of the shape?

cm

2 marks

21 **133 – *x* = 56**

What is the value of *x* in this equation?

Show your method

***x* =**

2 marks

Long multiplication/division: *If the answer is incorrect, award one mark for the formal method of long multiplication/ division which contains no more than one arithmetical error.*

Arithmetic:
Paper 1, Test 1

1. 943 *(N2) 1 mark*

2. 580 *(C7) 1 mark*

3. 7.5 *(F8) 1 mark*

4. 136 *(C7) 1 mark*

5. 1,776 *(C2) 1 mark*

6. 12 *(C6) 1 mark*

7. 583 *(C1) 1 mark*

8. 1.66 *(F8) 1 mark*

9. 72 *(C6) 1 mark*

10. $\frac{3}{8}$ *Accept equivalent fractions or an exact decimal equivalent. (F4) 1 mark*

11. 45 *(C6) 1 mark*

12. 174 *(C5) 1 mark*

13. 36 *(C5) 1 mark*

14. 24,800 *(C2) 1 mark*

15. 40,000 *(C6) 1 mark*

16. 178 *(C6) 1 mark*

17. 316 *(R2) 1 mark*

18. 7.28 *(F9) 1 mark*

19. $\frac{3}{7}$ *Accept equivalent fractions or an exact decimal equivalent. (F4) 1 mark*

20. 14,561 *(C2) 1 mark*

21. 1,193 *(C7) 1 mark*

22. 1.73 *(C2) 1 mark*

23. 1,708 *(C7) 2 marks*

24. 8.75 *(F1) 1 mark*

25. 245 *(C7) 1 mark*

26. $\frac{1}{27}$ *Accept equivalent fractions or an exact decimal equivalent. (F5) 1 mark*

27. 221 *(R2) 1 mark*

28. 83,286 *(C2) 1 mark*

29. 21,690 *(C7) 2 marks*

30. 20 $\frac{5}{8}$ *Accept equivalent fractions or an exact decimal equivalent. (F5) 1 mark*

31. 12 *(C9) 1 mark*

32. $\frac{2}{15}$ *Accept equivalent fractions or an exact decimal equivalent. (F5) 1 mark*

33. 1 $\frac{1}{15}$ *Accept equivalent fractions or an exact decimal equivalent. (F4) 1 mark*

34. 147 *(C7) 2 marks*

35. $\frac{7}{8}$ *Accept equivalent fractions or an exact decimal equivalent. (F4) 1 mark*

36. 48 *(C7) 2 marks*

Arithmetic:
Paper 1, Test 2

1. 160 *(C7) 1 mark*

2. 531 *(C1) 1 mark*

3. 6,528 *(C7) 1 mark*

4. 9.8 *(F8) 1 mark*

5. 303 *(N2) 1 mark*

6. 5,748 *(C2) 1 mark*

7.132 *(C6) 1 mark*

8. 3 *(C6) 1 mark*

9. 3.95 *(F8) 1 mark*

10. $\frac{3}{8}$ *Accept equivalent fractions or an exact decimal equivalent. (F4) 1 mark*

11. $\frac{2}{3}$ *Accept equivalent fractions or an exact decimal equivalent. (F4) 1 mark*

12. 85 *(C6) 1 mark*

13. 361 *(F9) 1 mark*

14. 324 *(C6) 1 mark*

15. 64 *(C5) 1 mark*

16. 24.16 *(C2) 1 mark*

17. 26,200 *(C6) 1 mark*

18. 31,700 *(C2) 1 mark*

19. 525 *(R2) 1 mark*

20. 17.05 *(F9) 1 mark*

21. 8 *(C6) 1 mark*

22. 9.87 *(F1) 1 mark*

23. 943 *(C7) 2 marks*

24. 13,663 *(C2) 1 mark*

25. 42,483 *(C2) 1 mark*

26. 410 *(C7) 2 marks*

27. $\frac{2}{15}$ *Accept equivalent fractions or an exact decimal equivalent. (F5) 1 mark*

28. 24 *(R2) 1 mark*

29. 2,273 *(C2) 1 mark*

30. $\frac{1}{8}$ *Accept equivalent fractions or an exact decimal equivalent. (F5) 1 mark*

31. 16 $\frac{4}{5}$ *Accept equivalent fractions or an exact decimal equivalent. (F5) 1 mark*

32. 108 *(C9) 1 mark*

33. $\frac{3}{32}$ *Accept equivalent fractions or an exact decimal equivalent. (F5) 1 mark*

34. 9,723 *(C7) 2 marks*

35. 42 *(C7) 2 marks*

36. $\frac{5}{12}$ *Accept equivalent fractions or an exact decimal equivalent. (F4) 1 mark*

Arithmetic:
Paper 1, Test 3

1. 10 *(C6) 1 mark*

2. 5.9 *(F8) 1 mark*

3. 56 *(C6) 1 mark*

4. 2,166 *(C7) 1 mark*

5. 3,607 *(N2) 1 mark*

6. 266 *(C7) 1 mark*

7. 1,944 *(C2) 1 mark*

8. 85 *(R2) 1 mark*

9. 377 *(C1) 1 mark*

10. 4.68 *(F8) 1 mark*

11. 35,600 *(C2) 1 mark*

12. 108 *(C6) 1 mark*

13. $\frac{3}{4}$ *Accept equivalent fractions or an exact decimal equivalent. (F4) 1 mark*

14. 246 *(C6) 1 mark*

15. 3,460 *(F9) 1 mark*

16. 121 *(C5) 1 mark*

17. $\frac{5}{12}$ *Accept equivalent fractions or an exact decimal equivalent. (F4) 1 mark*

18. 128 *(C6) 1 mark*

19. $\frac{2}{15}$ *Accept equivalent fractions or an exact decimal equivalent. (F5) 1 mark*

20. 7.35 *(F9) 1 mark*

21. $\frac{5}{8}$ *Accept equivalent fractions or an exact decimal equivalent. (F4) 1 mark*

22. 15,853 *(C2) 1 mark*

23. 2,074 *(C7) 1 mark*

24. 4.87 *(F1) 1 mark*

25. 12.59 *(C2) 1 mark*

26. 1,224 *(C7) 2 marks*

27. 28 *(C9) 1 mark*

28. 245 *(C7) 2 marks*

29. 24 $\frac{1}{2}$ *Accept equivalent fractions or an exact decimal equivalent. (F5) 1 mark*

30. 48 *(R2) 1 mark*

31. 568,667 *(C2) 1 mark*

32. 26,722 *(C7) 2 marks*

33. $\frac{2}{7}$ *Accept equivalent fractions or an exact decimal equivalent. (F5) 1 mark*

34. 74 *(C7) 2 marks*

35. 1 $\frac{1}{15}$ *Accept equivalent fractions or an exact decimal equivalent. (F4) 1 mark*

36. $\frac{4}{15}$ *Accept equivalent fractions or an exact decimal equivalent. (F5) 1 mark*

Arithmetic:
Paper 1, Test 4

1. 25 *(C5) 1 mark*

2. 1,122 *(C7) 1 mark*

3. 7.3 *(F8) 1 mark*

4. 60 *(C6) 1 mark*

5. 140 *(C7) 1 mark*

6. 407 *(C2) 1 mark*

7. 228 *(N2) 1 mark*

8. 4 *(C6) 1 mark*

9. 897 *(C1) 1 mark*

10. 1.44 *(F8) 1 mark*

11. 6/11 *Accept equivalent fractions or an exact decimal equivalent. (F4) 1 mark*

12. 310 *(F9) 1 mark*

13. 11 *(C6) 1 mark*

14. 29,500 *(C2) 1 mark*

15. 30,000 *(C6) 1 mark*

16. 22 *(C6) 1 mark*

17. 3 *(R2) 1 mark*

18. 18.42 *(F9) 1 mark*

19. 7.23 *(C2) 1 mark*

20. $\frac{3}{5}$ *Accept equivalent fractions or an exact decimal equivalent. (F4) 1 mark*

21. 7,013 *(C2) 1 mark*

22. 247 *(C7) 1 mark*

23. $\frac{41}{60}$ *Accept equivalent fractions or an exact decimal equivalent. (F5) 1 mark*

24. 1,435 *(C7) 2 marks*

25. 13.65 *(F1) 1 mark*

26. 36 *(C6) 1 mark*

27. 125 *(C7) 2 marks*

28. 13 *(R2) 1 mark*

29. 444,235 *(C2) 1 mark*

30. 20 *(F5) 1 mark*

31. 513,124 *(C2) 1 mark*

32. $\frac{3}{32}$ *Accept equivalent fractions or an exact decimal equivalent. (F5) 1 mark*

33. $3\frac{1}{4}$ *Accept equivalent fractions or an exact decimal equivalent. (F4) 1 mark*

34. 23 *(C7) 2 marks*

35. $\frac{21}{40}$ *Accept equivalent fractions or an exact decimal equivalent. (F4) 1 mark*

36. 3,625 *(C7) 2 marks*

Reasoning:
Paper 2, Test 1

1. 182; 122 *(N1) 1 mark*

2. 553 *(N3) 1 mark*

3. 5,015 *(N3) 1 mark*

4. Translation = B; Reflection = A *(P2) 2 marks*

5. 2160 cm^3 *(M8) 2 marks*

6. 7 hours 41 minutes *(M4) 1 mark*

7. 14 books *(C7) 2 marks*

8. 14° *(G4) 2 marks*

9. $\frac{3}{7} = \frac{9}{21}$

$\frac{1}{2} = \frac{11}{22}$

$\frac{5}{8} = \frac{10}{16}$

(F2) 2 marks

10. $\frac{3}{8}$ $\frac{2}{5}$ $\frac{4}{7}$ $\frac{8}{10}$ $\frac{5}{6}$

(F3) 2 marks

11. 22 cm *(G2) 2 marks*

12. 0.977 *(F10) 1 mark*

13. 150 grams *(R1) 2 marks*

14. a) $m = 102$; b) $n = 9$ *(A5) 2 marks (1 mark each)*

15. 216 cm^2 *(M7) 2 marks*

16. Triangular Pyramid: No. of faces: 4; No. of vertices: 4; No. of edges: 6; Square Pyramid: No. of faces: 5; No. of vertices: 5; No. of edges: 8 *(G2) 2 marks*

17. 36 cm *(G5) 2 marks*

18. 66° *(G4) 2 marks*

19. 13 *(S3) 2 marks*

20. 35 pupils *(R1) 2 marks*

Reasoning:
Paper 2, Test 2

1. 4 *(N3) 1 mark*

2. 8 *(C3) 1 mark*

3. 13 columns *(C3) 2 marks*

4. 8.5 cm *(G5) 1 mark*

5. 7 kg *(S3) 2 marks*

6. (1,12); (2,6); (3,4) *(C5) 2 marks*

7. $\frac{4}{5} = \frac{20}{25}$

$\frac{1}{9} = \frac{6}{54}$

$\frac{3}{5} = \frac{18}{30}$ *(F2) 2 marks*

8. 0.2 grams *(M9) 2 marks*

9. $x = 0.5$ or $\frac{1}{2}$ *(A1) 2 marks*

10. Maths *(P2) 2 marks*

11. $\frac{2}{8}$ $\frac{2}{5}$ $\frac{4}{10}$ $\frac{11}{15}$ $\frac{7}{9}$

(F3) 2 marks

12. *a* = 4, *b* = 12, *c* = 8 *(A5) 2 marks*

13. Triangular Prism: No. of faces: 5; No. of vertices: 6; No. of edges: 9 ; Rectangular Prism: No. of faces: 6; No. of vertices: 8; No. of edges: 12 *(G2) 2 marks*

14. D = (-9, -3), E = (0, 7) *(P3) 2 marks (1 mark each)*

15. 2 km *(M6) 2 marks*

16. a) £3.25 *(A2) 1 mark;* b) 20 badges *(A2) 2 marks*

17. a) £40; b) £100 *(S1) 2 marks (1 mark each)*

18. 841 *(N3) 1 mark*

19. Jack: 4:17 pm, Chloe: 4:41 pm *(M4) 2 marks (1 mark each)*

Reasoning:
Paper 2, Test 3

1. –7; +3 *(N5) 2 marks*

2. 1, 2, 5, 10 *(C5) 1 mark*

3. A = Reflection; B = Translation *(P2) 2 marks*

4. 503; 423 *(N2) 1 mark*

5. 13 packs *(M9) 2 marks*

6. 180,000; 184,000; 184,400 *(N4) 2 marks*

7. $\frac{2}{9}$ $\frac{4}{7}$ $\frac{7}{10}$ $\frac{3}{4}$ $\frac{11}{12}$

(F3) 2 marks

8. Area = 32 cm² ; Perimeter = 32 *cm (M7) 2 marks (1 mark each)*

9. £0.21 *(M9) 2 marks*

10. 0.4 *(F6) 1 mark*

11. 41, 43, 47 *(C5) 2 marks*

12. £4,285 *(F10) 2 marks*

13. $\frac{5}{16}$ *Accept equivalent fractions or an exact decimal equivalent. (F10) 2 marks*

14. 34 *(N3) 1 mark*

15. cone *(G2) 2 marks*

16. A = acute, B = reflex, C =obtuse *(G4) 2 marks*

17. 25 cm *(G5) 2 marks*

18. 475 ml *(R4) 2 marks*

19. 1.05 *(N3) 1 mark*

20. 152° *(G4) 2 marks*

Reasoning:
Paper 2, Test 4

1. 1 *(N3) 1 mark*

2. 27 cm *(M7) 2 marks*

3. -10; -21 *(N5) 2 marks*

4. 5:56 pm *(M4) 1 mark*

5. 2,059; 1,939 *(N2) 1 mark*

6. 0.96 metres *(M9) 2 marks*

7. £19.74 *(M3) 2 marks*

8. 75° *(G4) 2 marks*

9. 14; 24 *(C5) 1 mark*

10. 25% *(M9) 2 marks*

11. 12.5 *(F9) 1 mark*

12. £0.27 *(F10) 2 marks*

13. 320 ml (R1) 2 marks

14. *n* = $\frac{1}{4}$ or 0.25 *(A1) 2 marks*

15. 117 cm² *(M7) 2 marks*

16. 790,000, 793,000; 793,200 *(N4) 2 marks*

17. 7 books *(C7) 2 marks*

18. 75% *(F12) 2 marks*

19. 6.25 cm *(G5) 2 marks*

20. 5,068 grams *(M5) 2 marks*

Reasoning:
Paper 3, Test 1

1. 642,612; 654,612 *(N1) 1 mark*

2. 93 crayons *(C8) 1 mark*

3. 6 *(C3) 1 mark*

4. 6 *(F6) 1 mark*

5. £13.36 *(M9) 1 mark*

6. Decimal: 0.4; Percentage: 40% *(F11) 2 marks*

7. 75% *(F12) 2 marks*

8. 6, 20, 27 *(C5) 1 mark*

9. B = regular polygon; A and C = irregular polygon *(G2) 2 marks*

10. *n* = 3 *(A1) 2 marks*

11. 3,402, 4,417, 4,424 *(C5) 2 marks*

12. 60 cm *(M7) 2 marks*

13. A = obtuse, B = reflex, C = acute *(G4) 2 marks*

14. 80.5 metres *(M5) 1 mark*

15. (-5, 7) *(P2) 2 marks*

16. 19:35, 13:02, 00:06 *(M4) 2 marks*

17. cube *(G3) 2 marks*

18. 96 cm^2 *(M7) 2 marks*

19. rectangle = 2; isosceles triangle = 1; regular hexagon = 6 *(G2) 2 marks*

20. BA, BC = radius; AC = diameter *(G5) 2 marks*

21. 40 metres *(R3) 2 marks*

Reasoning:
Paper 3, Test 2

1. 16:32 *(M4) 1 mark*

2. 6 glasses *(C7) 1 mark*

3. 0.52, 520, 0.052 *(C6) 2 marks*

4. A = acute, B = obtuse, C = reflex *(G4) 2 marks*

5. Decimal: 0.8; Percentage: 80% *(F11) 2 marks*

6. $\frac{1}{6}$ *Accept equivalent fractions or an exact decimal equivalent. (F12) 2 marks*

7. rectangular prism *(G3) 2 marks*

8. 423.06, 423.116, 423.16, 423.186, 423.60 *(F8) 2 marks*

9. 1 *(F6) 1 mark*

10. 294 cm^2 *(M7) 2 marks*

11. 13 cm *(G5) 2 marks*

12. 2.8 *(F10) 1 mark*

13. 218,624, 219,524 *(N3) 1 mark*

14. *a* = 3 *(A1) 2 marks*

15. B = (9, 11); D = (3, 3) *(P3) 2 marks (1 mark each)*

16. 225, 450, 675 *(C5) 2 marks*

17. 19 seconds *(S3) 2 marks*

18. £4.28 *(M9) 2 marks*

19. square: 4; rhombus: 2, equilateral triangle:3 *(G2) 2 marks*

20. 2 cm *(M9) 2 marks*

Reasoning:
Paper 3, Test 3

1. £7.74 *(M9) 2 marks*

2. 46,251 pence *(M9) 1 mark*

3. 8 glasses *(M9) 2 marks*

4. 165, 132, 198 *(C5) 2 marks*

5. 28 *(F12) 2 marks*

6. $\frac{3}{4} = \frac{24}{32}$

$\frac{2}{5} = \frac{8}{20}$

$\frac{1}{6} = \frac{4}{24}$ *(F2) 2 marks*

7. 2.2 *(F7) 1 mark*

8. 152 *(C3) 2 marks*

9. 2,541, 2,491 *(N2) 1 mark*

10. 78° *(G4) 2 marks*

11. 2.4 *(F10) 1 mark*

12. 7 hours 9 minutes *(M4) 1 mark*

13. 6:15 pm *(M4) 2 marks*

14. (1, 20), (2, 10), (4, 5) *(C5) 2 marks*

15. -3, -8 *(N5) 2 marks*

16. £9.08 *(M9) 2 marks*

17. x = 0.75 or $\frac{3}{4}$ *(A1) 2 marks*

18. 318 cm^2 *(M7) 2 marks*

19. A: (5, 14), B: (15, 14) *(P3) 2 marks (1 mark each)*

20. C *(N3) 2 marks*

Reasoning:
Paper 3, Test 4

1. 0.022 kg *(M5) 1 mark*

2. 60 *(C3) 2 marks*

3. square = 4, rhombus = 2, equilateral triangle = 3 *(G2) 2 marks*

4. 4 hours 41 minutes *(M4) 1 mark*

5. 285, 303 *(N3) 1 mark*

6. 44 cm^2 *(M7) 2 marks*

7. Decimal: 0.25, Percentage: 25% *(F11) 1 mark*

8. 2,240 cm^3 *(M8) 2 marks*

9. 8 cups *(M5) 2 marks*

10. $\frac{3}{16}$ *Accept equivalent fractions or an exact decimal equivalent. (F12) 1 mark*

11. 44 cm *(M7) 2 marks*

12. Triangular pyramid: No. of faces: 4, No. of vertices: 4, No. of edges: 6; Triangular prism: No. of faces: 5, No. of vertices: 6, No. of edges: 9 *(G2) 2 marks*

13. $x = 108°$, $y = 72°$, $z = 72°$ *(G4) 2 marks*

14. 108, 180, 168 *(C5) 2 marks*

15. £3,407.90 *(M9) 2 marks*

16. 18 cm *(G5) 2 marks*

17. 665 *(N3) 1 mark*

18. 25th June *(M4) 1 mark*

19. 4 buses *(C7) 2 marks*

20. 72 cm *(M7) 2 marks*

21 $x = 77$ *(A1) 2 marks*